F

II

DEDICATION

To all the women and men who had to grow up in a single parent home, this is for you to know that you are not alone. Whatever goals you set for yourself you can achieve despite the obstacles and unfortunate circumstances! I am your #1 supporter.

TABLE OF CONTENTS

INTRODUCTION

Everything begins with our childhood, but we don't realize that until we are adults. From the moment we are born, everything and everyone that we encounter shapes our views, actions, decisions, dreams, fears, relationships, and much more. My story is not any different. Of course, I have a different journey because my path is mine; however, my story is like so many others in the world, especially women who were raised without fathers. There is this thing we carry around with us until we can face it. It lies in the shadows, ready to be revealed in whatever form best suits us. Once we have faced the thing deep inside of us, we are then able to unleash the best of ourselves and the world will take notice. While we are all affected in different ways and deal with things differently, once we have a breakthrough, we shine brighter than the sun. In my case, I unlock gifts that positively impact others and possess an aura that leaves precious stones in our path.

There are so many unknowns in life. Every one of us will encounter a variety of obstacles on different levels. The biggest issue is whether or not we have been given the proper tools to deal with life, especially the unknowns. Honestly, most of us are not given the correct tools to handle the things in life that may come our way. Being raised in a single parent home we tend to be limited in many ways. The main reason for this is because our single parents lacked many skills as they grew up, due to being raised in broken homes themselves. I know my mother was a good mother when it came to doing the best she could with what she had. Frankly, she still lacked in important areas to aid in my perception of the world and preparing me for the world which I will later go into more detail about in my book. She wasn't able to teach me some of the things I came to learn on my own volition because she was at a disadvantage during her childhood as well. I can't blame her for not having access to tools that I had growing up and with the new technology that continues to grow and allow me even more access to the world.

As I tell my story and give insight to empower you, my goal is to be a stepping stone for you, as well as let you know that you are not alone in this world of chaos that we live in today. We can teach ourselves to have peace of mind, regardless of what we go through. Once we reach a level of peace, then we can tackle anything that tries to get in our path as we go after our dreams. I am not an expert in how one should live his or her life. This book is only to share my story and give you some of the tools that I learned along the way. My only goal here is to help inspire, empower, and let you know that you are not alone.

CHAPTER 1
WHERE IT BEGAN

I grew up in Greenville, South Carolina. As a child, I remember having a good life. I have two brothers, I am the middle child. Looking back, there was nothing I lacked when it came to food, clothes, or shelter. I even remember that I had the best birthdays and Christmases with my family. Not only that, but I remember family events and spending time with my loved ones often. My mom has one brother and one sister. They both have children with whom we were remarkably close to growing up. I loved spending weekends and summers with my Auntie and her children the most. On top of that, I do have a few memories with my father, but those are very few. He was in my life until I was eleven years old. Although he was there until I was eleven years old, he was not present; or shall I say, he did not play the role one would expect a father to play.

One memory that comes to mind is when we stayed in this house on the west side of town. During this time I would have been around four or five years old.   I was standing on the porch waiting for my father to come back from taking out the trash so that we could play.   Time passed and I was left standing on the porch.   Not sure where my father disappeared to, but I just remember tears rolling down my face.   The next thing that happened was my mother came onto the porch to console me and take me back into the house.

As a child, I was always gifted in the academic area. From day 1 of school, I was always interested in learning and did exceedingly well.   Most kids would come home at five or six years old and need their parents' assistance with homework.   I was vastly different in this area because I would come home and do my homework without any assistance. My mother didn't have to ask me to do my homework and she never had to assist me with any of my assignments. I bet this was a blessing to her! School always came so natural to me.   It was my desire to learn. As a matter of fact, I was always more mature than the other kids in my age group, or it was just a God-given gift.   Regardless of what it was, I loved school and passed with flying colors.   I know some can relate, but there are others who may have had a more difficult time in school. No judgement, because this is typical as we are all made unique in God's image for a reason. The reason is much bigger than our eyes can see most of the time.

Another memory of my father is that we were outside playing catch with a plastic football. How do I remember this so well? During our game of catch, the ball hit me in the eye and it was the worst pain. I was around nine or ten years old. He told me, "Stop crying. You're okay, it didn't hurt you." Shortly after, I stopped crying. This is one of the extremely limited memories that I have of my father. We had fun that day together.

I also remember him taking the trash out one day. He told me, "Stay in the house. I will be right back and then we can play." The last thing I remember from that moment is seeing him walking to the end of the driveway and placing the trash in the receptacle. The thing is, he never came back that evening so that we could play. Once again I was left standing there crying and my mother came to the rescue again. These are the only memories I have of him. However, I do still remember his laugh and him cooking for us a couple of times.

Now that I am older, I understand why he abandoned me this way. Once I was of age, I learned that he was on drugs throughout my life. So instead of tending to his daughter who needed him so dearly, he was out chasing a high that I could not fulfill. During it all he had no idea about the damage he was causing. I was a little girl who needed and wanted her father. Every time we were supposed to have daddy-daughter time, he always bailed on me. Growing up, this is what I witnessed. As I grew up, I thought that is what men do. It was ingrained in my head that I wasn't good enough for my father to be in my life so how could I be good enough for any man to be a part of my life? It was an innate thing that was inside of me and I had no idea that I was fighting something within me that would shape my perception of relationships with males in such a drastic way.

At the age of eleven, my parents split up and we moved to Taylors, South Carolina. My mother met my stepfather and he seemed to play a better role than my father. As far as my father being in my life, that didn't change much. If anything, the distance only grew. He was probably still on drugs because he had the same behavioral patterns.

There were many times he was supposed to come and get me and my baby brother for the weekend, but when the day came, he wouldn't show up or even call. There were times he would contact me at the last minute and cancel our plans. Can you imagine the hurt that I felt as a little girl?

I remember this one incident where we were supposed to go shopping. We were going to the mall to buy me a coat. You can't even imagine the excitement I felt that entire week. When the day finally came, it didn't happen. Now, he did swing by and drop the money off so that I could still buy a coat, but he wasn't going to be sharing the experience with me. Oh, how I remember crying my eyes out to my mother. She was terribly upset and hurt to see her little girl in such pain. The first man who should have been my protector and provider was neither one. So how was I supposed to know how a man is meant to treat you?

Many things that I learned growing up were mainly through observation. Somehow, I have always been wise beyond my years. Although I didn't have my father to teach me directly how a man should treat me, he indirectly taught me what not to allow in my life. Just from observing and analyzing life for myself, I knew that I didn't want a man in my life who breaks promises, hurts me, and doesn't make me his priority. These are things I experienced with my father and it was non-negotiable when it came to men. Going through life, I chose things that I felt were a good fit in my life and eliminated things that seemed to be a hindrance.

Until I was maybe twelve years of age, he dated this lady. She was genuinely nice and allowed me to come over a couple of times. To be honest, when I went to visit, I spent more time building a bond with her and getting to know her than my father. He was just as absent as he had been all those years. So eventually those visits came to an end, because the purpose was to spend time with my father and that was not happening.

Thoughts ran through my head, "How could my father not want to be in my life?" Being the person I was, I never shared these feelings that were brewing around inside of me. To be honest, when I was a little girl, I didn't know how to fully process my feelings. Not only that, but I was an introvert. So, I tended to internalize my feelings and not deal with them head on. As I grew older, this trait about me did not change. If anything, I became more introverted and shared my emotions less and less.

At this point in my life, I was approaching my teenage years. My mother was quite fed up with the disappointment my father caused for me and my baby brother so many times. I do know she never placed him on child support or so much as spoke negatively about him around us. His ultimatum (which I found out when I became of age) was to either keep his word to me and my baby brother, or do not come around getting our hopes up to only let us down and leave my mother with the mess to clean up. That is exactly what happened. I did not hear from him for years.

As time went on, I really suppressed how I felt about him not being in my life. Maybe at first I did not know how to properly express my feelings. I chose not to share them, not even with my best friend at the time. Deep down, it played a major role in my life and ate me up on the inside. I didn't even know how to express this to my mother. Honestly, she grew up without a father too. She did the best she could do as far as protecting me, her only daughter. Things left unsaid or things that are unknown will only go so far. How was I to know that it would be better for me to face my father abandoning us? How was I to know that I needed to talk things out with someone? How was I to know that I wasn't the only little girl who was fatherless? This journey was a tough one and honestly, I do not believe I was prepared for it, but God equipped me very well with everything I needed to overcome so much. I just want my story and my journey to help others like myself. Being fatherless isn't the end of the world, once you learn how to deal with that loss in a healthy manner.

All these questions I had running through my head. Even as the only girl in my family, I didn't necessarily have what I would call a close relationship with my mother; or should I say, I wasn't a "momma's girl." I don't recall her sitting down with me having conversations that mothers should have with their daughters. She never explained to me why my father wasn't around. She never talked to me about how a lady should carry herself or how a man should treat her. If my memory serves correctly, she didn't really play with me much or create that mother-daughter bond with me, because she was always working. This did not mean she loved me any less because I know she always has and always will. My mother is my biggest supporter throughout everything. I mean, as a single parent, she had to provide for my brothers and myself. The time that we could have spent together, she was working and most times at two jobs. I knew that she loved me, but she wasn't able to give the tools I needed from her. Her mind was probably set in "survival mode." Survival mode means that she only knew how to provide for us and do the best she could to make sure we had a place to stay, food, and clothes.

Please understand that our parents are not to blame when it comes to lacking in certain areas. They are human as well. Their childhood was quite different from ours and they were not equipped with the proper tools of life as well. Just like we are faced with hardships, obstacles, and disadvantages, so were our parents. I know that my mother was growing up. Do your best to not blame your single parent for not being able to provide you with everything you need in life; the reality is that he or she lacked in many areas as well. However, acknowledge that he or she did their best and despite what you did lack, you will still manage to succeed in life. Trust me, I have succeeded against all odds.

I'm pretty sure some of you are able to relate to this idea. Many of us who grew up in single parent homes must deal with this. They give you the necessities, but anything more, you must learn on your own or outside of the house. Learning things outside the house can end up good or bad. Life boils down to choices and the choices you make can impact you negatively or positively. Luckily for me, I took a positive route and I want many of you to do the same.

CHAPTER 2

UNFOLDING MY LIFE AS A TEEN

School was something I always loved. It came quite easy for me. Since kindergarten, I didn't need assistance with homework and I flourished throughout school, always getting good grades. This is something that kept me grounded throughout everything I went through. Embracing education was something I enjoyed. I went to school got a good education at Riverside High School and made some good connections along the way.

Now, going through school I was bit of a loner. I mean I conversed with many of my classmates and a few of the people that lived in my neighborhood; however, I kept to myself overall. I was unique in the sense that I didn't need validation from a group or clique while in school. I always walked to the beat of my own drum and it worked in my favor in many ways. My grades were always above a 3.5 GPA and I never got into any trouble, which really made my mother proud.

Although I didn't play sports in school, I always had a

passion for dance. Growing up, I could naturally dance. Thinking back to my childhood I could choreograph dances at a noticeably young age. This was a hobby I enjoyed alone and with my cousins as well. Not only would I choreograph dances, but we would pretend we were a singing group, which was fun. Dance is something that really stuck with me as I grew up. My Auntie would even have me dance for her friends whenever I was at her place because I was so talented. In school, my extracurricular activities were none other than dance and step team. If you don't know what a step team is, it's similar to dance, but a step team doesn't have to have music. We created music with our feet and hands by putting beats together and synchronizing our moves as well. My passion for music only grew the older I got.

Having an outlet is good for you. Whatever you love to do or have a passion for, stick with it. This can help you through tough times, as well as assist you with finding what you really want to do in life. Whether it's dance, sports, music, video games, writing, poetry, or whichever your outlet is, this can help you get out of some dark places and keep you on track for what you are really meant to accomplish in life. I can say that dance, music, exercise, meditation, and writing are my outlets. You can have a few avenues to express yourself in a healthy way. These things helped me in the darkest hours of my life, and believe me, they will help you too.

Everything seemed to be going well for me as I sailed through school with minimal storms. Little did I know, I was unconsciously dealing with the lack of a father. Emotionally, I was suffering, yet I didn't even realize that it was affecting me in such a tremendous way. It mainly affected my relationships with males that I was in a serious relationship with during these times. Looking back, I was blind to the toll it was taking on me. Socially and academically, I was excelling in life at the time, at least I thought so. I was on track for graduating and going to college, as I always dreamed of doing.

During my junior year of high school, many of the emotional things I had been dealing with caught up to me. I became isolated from everyone, even my best friends. My mom was always there for me, but I didn't feel comfortable talking to her; plus, as a teenage girl, we really bumped heads. There were times I didn't even want to live with her. It was all part of the emotional distress that I was going through. So as time went on, I became even more isolated and very depressed. Earlier that year, which would have been 2006, I lost a close friend to a brain aneurism. That hit me hard because we were close. Although I was able to attend the—wait—I wasn't able to attend the funeral because my mom felt that I could not handle it emotionally. Anyhow, I spent most of my time staying busy after that with school, work, and step team. I believe keeping myself occupied was an escape for me. That only lasted a few months though because depression crept up on me like a scary monster in the night.

At first, it began with me becoming very withdrawn from my friends and family. Then, the things I loved to do such as dance, write poetry, and listen to music became things I no longer had an interest in doing at this time. Honestly, things unraveled for me. I became suicidal and wanted to kill myself whenever I was awake. So, during my free time, I slept as much as possible because that is the only way I could keep my mind off of the pain that I was feeling deep down. I would take a bunch of over the counter pills, hoping I would never wake up. Of course, the next day I would awake with just as much agony on the inside than the day before.

Since taking pills didn't help take the pain away, I began cutting myself on the wrist with a razor blade. I would hide it by wearing long sleeves, jackets, cardigans, or a coat so no one could see it. Somehow, my mother knew something was going on with me. One day, she came into my room while I was asleep and saw the fresh cuts on my arms. She was devastated, she had no clue what to do. She received information about a hotline and called it. Apparently, they told her to keep an eye on me and if she finds fresh cuts to admit me to the hospital. Well, at the time, I didn't know that she received this information. I continued cutting myself because that was my cry for help. When she came into my room the next day to check on me, she found fresh cuts and she admitted me to the hospital.

This was a very emotional day and was a turning point for me. I felt so lost and didn't fully understand what was happening to me. All the way to the hospital, I cried because I didn't want to go, but she gave me no choice.

Once I got there, the doctors admitted me to the hospital because I was a threat to myself. The circumstances infuriated me. I didn't want to be in a hospital with them telling me what to do. I had never been through anything like this in my life. At the time, I felt like my mother was being unjust. Any control I previously had was instantly snatched away from me.

During my two-week stay at the hospital, I went through a lot and learned a lot. My boyfriend at the time seemed to be supportive, because my mother would call me with him on three-way the entire time I was there. My daily routine was to eat breakfast, lunch and dinner, partake in group therapy sessions with teens who were suffering from depression as well, do my school work that was sent over, and partake in any activities they had for us. They controlled your entire day. This experience really opened my eyes to life in a different way. The last thing I wanted was to let someone else control my life because I have always been an independent, ambitious, and strong-minded girl. There was an incident while I was hospitalized when they served some food that I didn't eat. They told me I had to eat it or I wouldn't get my dessert. This agitated me because they were trying to force me to eat something that I never eat. My agitation escalated and they had to give me a sedative to relax me. At that moment, I knew that I really had to take heed of the things they were teaching us. I had to throw my stubborn ways out the window if I wanted to go home sooner rather than later.

Two weeks later, I was finally home. Being there taught me how to deal with my emotions in an extremely healthy manner. But, I was not ready for the next event that was about to happen. My boyfriend couldn't handle the things that were going on with me, so he broke up with me. Of course, my feelings were hurt; but, to be honest our relationship had been rocky anyway. Plus, we were young. So, looking back, I can understand how that would be too much for a teenage boy to handle.

My healing process was far from over. Part of being released from the hospital meant that I had to go to therapy as well as visit a psychiatrist. These sessions went very well for me. I was finally able to give everything going on inside of me a voice. Not only that, but I was able to talk to someone without judgement. My therapy sessions went very well, but my therapist got promoted and I was given a new therapist. The new therapist did not seem as relatable to me, and my sessions with her didn't last long.

After that, I got a mentor who would pick me up and take me out to different places to have our sessions. Those sessions were very progressive. During this time, I was on an antidepressant, but I hated taking medicine. Yes, the antidepressant was effective for me for a few months, but I was incredibly determined to wean myself off of it because I didn't want to be dependent on medicine to feel better. The first time I took myself off the medication, it did not go so well. I felt even more depressed than before and I had to get back on it. With all my mentor sessions and being able to get to a healthy state of mind, I was able to successfully wean myself off the medication later.

For me, this was one of the pivotal moments in my life. I learned so many things about myself during this time. I was much stronger than I thought. Each day I fought harder for myself, so that I could have my sanity at such a young age. Dealing with a plethora of emotions, but still being able to get back to a common ground. During this time, I felt like I went through a whirlwind for about two years. I learned that there are people who love and care for me in ways I didn't know. Also, that there are people in the world who suffer from different issues and some may share the same issues as yours. I was fortunate enough to get the help I needed because of all the support that surrounded me. My support system and my temperance helped all my ill feelings and emotional distress dissipate. At the end of all of this, I came out better and stronger for my next chapter of life as I graduated from high school and went to college. Regardless of the struggles I faced by my father not being in my life, I graduated high school with flying colors.

Seeking help through therapy or a counselor can do more good than harm. I highly suggest therapy when it comes to dealing with different life issues. Our loved ones can sometimes allow their emotions to get in the way of what they deem as best for us. Of course, we know that we can get in our own way as well, because there are times when we are in situations and we allow our emotions to cloud our judgement. I am here to tell you an unbiased opinion from someone, such as a therapist, can help change your life in a tremendous way. The main reason is, a therapist approaches your issues with objectivity, which in turn gives a new perspective on things that you are dealing with in your life. Going to therapy helped change my life and I am 99% sure that it can do the same for you. You must have an open mind for it to work though.

CHAPTER 3
A NEW LEAF

Going to college was always one of my main goals in life. Throughout my high school years, I always maintained great grades. To be honest, school was a breeze for me. I went to class, studied, and made good grades. It was as easy as breathing. Anyway, I was accepted to USC Upstate, which is in Spartanburg, SC. I was ecstatic for this next chapter in my life! One of the peculiar things about me is that I always knew what I wanted to do with my life, and that was to be a successful entrepreneur. So, I majored in Business Administration and Management. The first two years of college were easy because it was like high school all over again, and I passed my classes with flying colors.

I was not like most of my peers. I commuted to college during my entire four years because I was an introvert and I didn't like people in my space unless there was a greater purpose at stake. For me, living on campus and having strangers as roommates was not an option. Fortunately for me, my older brother purchased my first car for me so that I could have reliable transportation and not have to be concerned with unnecessary bills. It was such a blessing to have an older brother like him. This really relieved me of a burden during school.

Not only was I a full-time student, but I partook in other extracurricular activities as well. On top of working two jobs, during my first year I also assisted my former step team with routines. After that, I took ballet classes for a while. Then, I took hip-hop dance classes at a studio in Mauldin, SC. I have enjoyed dancing since I was a little girl. Since I was in school at the time, the owner set up a deal with me where I would assist as a tutor in her after school program. In exchange, I did not have to worry about paying tuition each month. An unbelievable blessing I would say, because not only did I have a passion for dance, but I loved working with children. This exchange was the best of both worlds for me. This lasted for a while, until I decided to take on an internship on campus as a Student Administrative Assistant during my junior year of college. Basically, I set up on-campus events, such as career fairs, and communicated with faculty, students, and employers who partnered with our school.

Looking back, college seemed to fly by. During my sophomore year I had a moment of growth. As a teenager I had a bad attitude for some reason, it could relate to my father not being around and other factors as well. When I was nineteen years old, my mother said something to me one day that really resonated with my spirit: "I don't know why you are so prideful, you need to work on that." Over the years, my mother told me a variety of things that I didn't listen to, especially as a teenager. This time was different for me though, because those words resonated through me like an echo. At this time I was very prideful; however, I took notice at how it affected the way I wanted to be viewed by others. So, I prayed about it and took steps to fix this flawed part of me.

My mother did the best she could raising us by herself. I mean, I was her second child to attend college. The things I really lacked came from my father not being in my life, as well as a few missed steps with my mother. During my sophomore year of college, I dated this guy. We hit it off well and things took off between us a bit faster than anyone else I dated. When it ended, it ended badly. After each breakup, I started to feel like maybe things not working out was my fault. Really, it was the absence of my father that played a background role in all my relationships. Although I was quite successful in many areas, such as school, I wasn't as successful in relationships. Maybe it was the theory that your first love should be your father, which I didn't have at all. Possibly because a father is the one who teaches his daughter how she should be loved by another man and how a man should treat her. Since I never had any of these things, I taught myself what was acceptable or not. I think I did a great job at building character and integrity as a woman raised by a single mother.

As time carried on into my junior and senior year of college, I felt so accomplished. I was fulfilling a second goal of mine. My first goal was to graduate high school, and now I would be graduating college soon. Looking back to May of 2012, I couldn't believe the time was coming for my college graduation. The determination, self-discipline, and ambition that drove me was allowing me to gain the success I wanted for many years. At that point in life, I felt accomplished, like my life was on track. I felt that I beat all odds. Not only was I making strides for being raised in a single parent home, but I was the first girl in my family to attend college and graduate. Plus, I didn't have any kids and never got pregnant. I was doing very well for myself.

Once you set your mind on something, no obstacle is big enough to get in your way. The life I was given was beyond my control. However, my control began in my mind. You can succeed and accomplish anything as long as you don't hold yourself back. Most importantly, do not allow circumstances to become a crutch and hold you back from your goals. Instill success in your mind and you will be amazed at the great things that you can overcome in your journey of life. My mother wasn't rich by far. So, if I can accomplish my goals with the things I endured along the way and my limited resources, trust me, your goals are only a thought away, and persistence is the key to unlocking your dreams.

CHAPTER 4
ON TO THE NEXT

After graduating college, I knew I had to begin my career somewhere. During this time, I was a Shift Leader at Hardees, which is a management position. I loved the job and have always excelled at customer service. As much as I loved the job, it was time for me to move on to something with a greater salary and a place where my skill set would be acknowledged more.

Let me tell you that life is not easy, but it is also not as complicated as some humans make it seem. Throughout my years of schooling, I was influenced by my mother, teachers, peers, associates, and other people I met along the way. Some of the people were helpful when it came to me deciding the path I wanted to take in life and others showed me the path I did not want to take in life. Not only that, but I felt like once I graduated college, life was not like the picture that my mother, teachers, and others had painted in my head. It was like my fairy tale story was shattered. There was so much more to life than what

I was taught growing up and it didn't hit me until I graduated college. At this point, I started to experience life for myself with a different perspective.

Just thinking back, I can remember that going to college was the goal. That is what my teachers instilled in us. Then, after getting a good education, you could go into the real world and get whatever job you wanted. A big piece of information was missing that neither my mother nor my teachers taught me about all those years. That information was: college is not the only route to success in life. Life has limitless opportunities which all begin in the mind. If you think that your life has limits, then it does; but, if you believe life is limitless, then it is. Everything starts in the mind based on the way that you think. This is when I began to change my mindset. I started to figure out life for myself and stopped living life through other people's eyes. Doing your own research can be the best way, in most cases, when deciphering what is best for you.

Although I found a good job working in a loan servicing company, I knew that God had greater plans in store for me. Growing up, I was always very different than my peers. At a young age, I was quite mature. I knew what I wanted out of life and knew who I was. There was no one or nothing that could stand in my way despite the obstacles I had to overcome throughout life thus far.

During this time, life was rather good after college. I was staying at home with truly little debt at the time. On top of working my day job at the loan servicing company, I was also a bartender. Both jobs added so much value to my life in quite different ways. At the loan servicing company, I was one of the best analysts on my team. I got to meet some great people that the company did business with from different parts of the United States. Not only that, but I was learning about an industry that I did not know anything about. My title was Remarketing Analyst. The job entailed sending cars to auction after they had been repossessed from customers who defaulted on their car loans, or voluntarily gave the car back because the customer could not make payments any longer. Our contact with customers was minimal. We spent most of our time building rapport with auctioneers and repo agents around the nation. Honestly, I loved the job because I was learning new things everyday about an industry that I definitely was not knowledgeable about at the time. Connections were another big thing with the job. The auctioneers connected with me on Linked In to keep in touch as well as continue to build our relationship. These are connections that I was able to build and maintain for years to come.

Building connections was sort of new to me at this time because I didn't really do much networking while in school. I was an introvert and preferred to stay to myself. I never hung in groups or cliques as it just wasn't my thing. So, being in this industry really helped me learn to make connections and build relationships. Trust me, these are lifelong skills that I didn't even realize I would need.

As a bartender, I had to step out of my shell too. Mixing drinks and the customer service part was amazingly easy for me since I already had about six years of customer service experience working at Hardees. Now, I had to learn to deal with not only vast personalities, but a whole different mindset that customers and people I worked with had as well. These customers were different because they would be at the bar for hours, and as they drank, they wanted to have conversations about a multitude of topics. This was different for me because, like I stated previously, I was an introvert. So, I didn't socialize much with random strangers before this. After a while, I grew to like the bartending job because it was pulling me out of my shell. It taught me how to deal with different personalities, and I learned that I was enthralled with meeting new people because they all had so many different perspectives in life. Learning is something that has always elated me. I have this thirst for knowledge that never seems to get quenched.

Some of the reasons that I was such an introvert were that I did not want people getting close to me. Yes, I had about three close friends growing up, but outside of them I was extremely cautious. To be honest, my father being absent in my life may have played a part. However, the jobs I worked, as well as going to college, helped me see life in a new light. It showed me that there were a few people that could be trusted. At the same time, I still had trust issues, especially with men. I am certain the trust issues with men stems from the lack of my father's presence in my life.

As life passed, each day taught me so much about being out in the world. There is more to life than what they teach you in school, or even what you learn at home. In the back of my mind, I knew that. I taught myself so many things based on observation and doing my own research. Yet, there was much more to life than my mind could fathom.

CHAPTER 5
GRASPING WHAT LIFE HAS TO OFFER

The biggest role my father could have played in my life was teaching me how a man should treat me. With my father being absent, I did not have that luxury growing up and it affected me in ways that I could not have anticipated. From high school through college, I had been in relationships that failed and at the time I couldn't understand why. Maybe I was broken from the lack of my father's presence, or maybe the men I attracted weren't right for me, or it could be a combination of both. All I knew was, the dating scene wasn't that great for me.

During my junior year of college, I met this guy who seemed to be very nice and we hit it off very well. By the time I graduated college, we decided to take things to the next step as far as being in a committed relationship. Things seemed fine for the first two years; I thought he would be the one, but all of that changed shortly after he asked me to move in with him. Let me be the one to tell you that I had never lived with anyone outside of my family. The only people I ever lived with were my mother and two brothers. So, this was new for me and exciting. Of course, by the time he had asked me to move in with him we had been seeing each other for two years already; hint: I was in love at this point. Trust me, I did not know how to respond exactly when he completely changed after us living together for a short period of time.

All my life, I had been this person who knew who she was and what she wanted. Growing up without a father was difficult because they are supposed to teach you about men. Your father is supposed to be your first love and show you how a man should love you and treat you. Since I didn't have this, I had to learn along the way in ways that really damaged me emotionally and mentally.

I am here to tell you that being raised in a single parent home is a major obstacle within itself. We do not get to choose the circumstances we are born into. Trust me, I know this firsthand. Things may seem tough sometimes, and you may even feel alone from time to time. I want you to know that at some point in life, you do have choices. You get to choose the path you want to take, despite your circumstances. Frankly, playing the victim is not going to get you very far in life. The best thing that worked for me is having God's grace and being able to maneuver through the roadblocks that I faced along the way. Having a strong support system also helps, whether it's a relative, friend, therapist, mentor, or whomever. Let me tell you that the roadblocks made me better—resilient—if I must say so myself. They made me stronger and a better person for not only myself, but for others who are in my life.

Going back to my relationship, there were so many things I tolerated that I should not have. Honestly, I probably should not have stayed with him for as long as I did. We ended up being together for almost five years. I know what you are thinking, "Why be with someone that long when things weren't working out?" The thing is, I kept telling myself that he was going through a phase and that it was only temporary. The fact of the matter is that it wasn't temporary, and it only got worse from there. Not to go into any specific details, I dealt with lies, cheating, disrespect, lack of support, and being unappreciated.

I am here to tell you that no man or woman should put

himself or herself through such a situation. A huge part could be that my father wasn't in my life to show me how a man should treat me. All I wanted was to be accepted and loved by this man at any cost. A voice in my head told me that this was not what love was supposed to be, but my heart could not detach from him. So, I put up with this relationship until I was completely empty. After pouring everything I had into someone who did not pour back into me, I was completely empty. I had lost myself in this relationship. Regret is something that I do not have because I came out of this situation a better person, although it took time for me to heal and allow myself to grow. There is always an upside, even in the bad situations that we go through.

Circling back around to the choices that we make in life. There are many things in life that are beyond our control, as well as many people. The only person we can fully control is ourselves. Once you can master self-discipline you will feel the power that you have to truly take control of your life. Although most situations we are not able to control, we are able to control how we respond to things and people, as well as what we allow ourselves to be a part of. You have so much power that most of you have not tapped into. Search deep within yourself and unleash the power that you were born with. Trust me, it is deep down in your soul waiting to be revealed.

CHAPTER 6
SILVER LINING

In the midst of the relationship that I told you about in the previous chapter, I was able to start my first business back in June, 2014. This is one of the things I always dreamed about doing. The type of business I wanted to start changed over the course of the years; however, I always knew I wanted to be an entrepreneur back in middle school. Of course, I wanted to be a cosmetologist back then as well because I loved doing hair. Then, in high school I wanted to be a professional dancer, or shall I say choreographer, because dance was always a passion of mine. I didn't know what the future held for me and I still don't.

After college, God put it in my spirt to start my own business. I graduated with a Bachelor's degree in Business Administration and Management, so I knew how to do a business plan and the basic research that I needed to complete before starting it. I remember going to work and thinking that I wanted to finally open a dance studio.

My second passion is kids. I have always enjoyed working with kids. Even when I was in middle school and high school, I was always the babysitter. Looking back, kids have always naturally been drawn to me and we bond very well. So, to me, it only made sense that I open a dance studio.

Once I began my research, I came across something that really piqued my interest. The childhood obesity rate in South Carolina was around 18% and this was a growing issue in our nation at the time, and still is. For some reason, this really stood out to me and captured my heart. Instead of the dance studio, I decided to open a kids' gym. First things first, I had to come up with a catchy name for the business. I remember racking my brain at work on my breaks, during downtime, and when I was off. One day, I was talking to one of my coworkers from another department about it. He was interested in my dream and a few days later, he came back with a business name for me: KidzFusion. I was elated. The name was perfect to me as it just screamed fun for kids. That was the beginning for me to start working on my business plan.

The idea began in 2012. I put the business plan together by myself, based off the skills I learned in my business classes from college. I already had a good bit of money saved because I was good at that sort of thing during this time. After doing some networking, I was able to find a graphic designer to create my logo. After a few attempts, he nailed it. Then in June of 2014, I registered my business and began to do the work to get my name out there.

This was a new world for me out of the gate. In school, we discussed different businesses and how to start a business, but doing it firsthand was another beast. Stepping out of my shell was like having an anxiety attack because I had to learn how to be an extrovert in order to network and go up to strangers to convince them to do business with me. I won't lie, I was so frightened at first. This was new terrain for me. It is easy to get up Monday through Friday and punch the clock for someone else. When you are building a business from the ground up though, there is so much work to be done. Whether the business fails or succeeds falls on you. Talk about the pressure that was on me. My vision was intact and there was no one or nothing that was going to get in my way.

Let me be frank: it was not an easy journey at the beginning. There is this lady I worked with at my job who connected me with a lady who had a dance studio. She pretty much allowed me to use her students to do my kids' fitness since I was just starting my business. Of course, I was doing it for free so that I could get exposure. One thing I will tell you about starting a business is that you definitely have to give to receive. Sometimes, you have to give more than you bargained for; but, it pays off in the end.

From there, I began networking and attending different events to get my business out there. I opened social media accounts which I did not have before I started my business. All of this was new to me, especially the marketing side of things. All I can say is that hard work truly pays off and that God placed the right people in my path at the right times to assist me along the way. It is crazy because my original business plan was to open a kids' fitness gym. During the process, I decided to turn it into a mobile kids' fitness program because it was more cost-efficient and it seemed to work out for me at the time. Instead of worrying about overhead costs, all I had to do was present my program to different daycares, churches, schools, and community centers to convince them to let me perform my services at their facilities. I never imagined that I would be a part of such an amazing movement by helping kids be active.

Let me tell you that I began to build my empire while in the toxic relationship that I discussed in the previous chapter. He was not supportive of my dreams. Somehow, I was able to block out all the negativity and put all my positive energy into the business I always dreamed about building. It seemed like the worse the relationship became, the more focused I was on my business. The relationship was like a curse and a blessing all wrapped in one. Through everything that I was going through in that relationship, my goals never wavered. I suppose my passion, drive, and ambition outweighed any obstacle that I came across. For that, I am forever grateful because that is a gift that very few people in this world are blessed with. Some things will come into your life to really break you down. You control if a situation will break you down or build you up stronger than you were before. This only proves that everything starts in the mind, and the mind is stronger than you even know. All you have to do is program your mind for the right things that will help you excel in whatever you want to do in life.

You may be wondering why I even mentioned the relationship in the first place. It was to show you that nothing can stop you from reaching your goals but YOU. From day one, I was doomed because my father was not in my life. At that point, I could have allowed that to consume me and take another path in life. I didn't though, I stayed the course. I excelled in high school and college by getting good grades and graduating from both. Then, this toxic relationship could have been the breaking point out of everything else I endured before then as well. Did I allow it to break me? Absolutely not, I kept a leveled head and pushed through so that I could build my legacy.

CHAPTER 7
KEEPING YOUR EYE ON THE PRIZE

Life is quite peculiar. I wish I had all the answers for you to help things go more smoothly. What I do have is sound advice based off my experiences thus far in life. It may not be the exact answer for you, but I am sharing my story with you because it has helped me become the person that I am today. Honestly, I don't know who I would be if things happened differently in my life. I am a big believer in Karma, and a believer in things aligning in your life just as they should. Now, I am not saying that everything that happens is going to be sunshine and fresh flowers, but I am saying that even the storms come to catapult you to the next chapter or next level in your life. In my opinion, the pain we endure throughout life molds us for the true gifts of life. Everything we go through is part of the bigger picture of our life. To help us become who God genuinely wants us to be, you must be self-aware of what's going on within yourself and fully tune in to your inner spirit to grasp all that life has for you.

I could be dishonest and tell you that life gets easier with time. Honestly, it does not get easier, and there are all sorts of unexpected hurdles along the way. You may not be prepared for every single obstacle that comes your way however, you can learn how to navigate through life healthily. The biggest way to do this is to find happiness and peace within yourself. I give you this type of advice because it has changed my life. Naturally, there are always going to be hardships to face, decisions to be made, disappointments, heartbreaks, setbacks, and all sorts of unexpected things with yourself, family, friends, business associates and colleagues. The key to overcoming all of this is being able to teach yourself how to always be in a healthy headspace. No, this is not easy as it takes continuous work daily. If you want to accomplish great things in life, it is worth the time and effort.

Another big piece of advice I would like to offer is to always have faith in God. God will bring you out of the darkest places, pull you from the toughest situations, be there for you when it seems that you're all out of options, listen to you when you don't have an earthly ear, and allow tremendous things to take place in your life. The only way all of this will happen is to believe in God. For those of you who may have a difficult time with this, start by praying and meditating. Prayer and meditation are such powerful tools; I know this firsthand. Throughout my life when things seemed to get tough, God always sees me through to the other, brighter side. Also, you can seek assistance through a spiritual mentor or by fellowshipping at church. These are great resources to help you through life as well. Another amazing tool is to read, because there is always someone who is going through a similar situation or has been through it in some point in their life. This will help you analyze your life issues and get on the right path to making the best decisions for you.

Therapy can also help you in more ways than you know. I went to therapy back in high school when I was faced with depression. Then, I went to therapy again when I was in my long-term relationship that I told you about in a previous chapter. Please, if you have a negative connotation about therapy in your head, consider being more open-minded about it. I hear some people say that they don't want to go to therapy because they don't want to talk to a stranger about their personal business. The truth is that this is an experienced, non-biased individual, who can help you sort out any issues that you may be dealing with in life. Seeing a therapist can give you a healthier outlook on the issues you are dealing with, and it can give you a fresh perspective that you did not even consider. Many times, when we talk to our family or friends about certain situations, they will not always give us the best, sound advice because they are emotionally attached. This is why a therapist is an excellent third party to reach out to.

My final piece of advice is: always be true to yourself. As you go through life, there will be people who try to tell you what is best for you or even how you should do certain things in your life, whether it's related to careers, personal relationships or any area of your life. Now I am not saying that you cannot accept advice from people, just make sure it is sound advice that makes sense for your life. Otherwise, always keep God in everything that you do. Pray about your moves and decisions in life as well as about advice that people give you. Never take what someone tells you and run with it. Always conduct your own research because some people do not have your best interest at heart. There are some people who are wolves in sheep's clothing. You must beware of these people! God will put all kinds of people, good and bad, in our paths to shape us for what he truly has in store for us. I am letting you know to be aware and use all of the tools you have at your fingertips. The biggest thing to go by is your intuition. We all have intuition, but it is up to you whether you use it or ignore it. I am here to tell you that my intuition is always right, literally 100% of the time.

In closing, I want you to know that you are never alone. Despite the hand you may have been dealt, there is still sunshine on the other side of that storm. My purpose in life is to be a helper. That means I have this desire to make change in the world and help those who are truly in need in different communities and various walks of life. It is truly a blessing to be the selfless person that I am, especially when it means that I can make a difference in just one person's life. Changing just one life can impact the world in more ways than you know. I am here to change as many lives as my spirit allows me to, as long as I have the tools to do so. Remember that I love you regardless of if you are a stranger, foe, or friend. At the end of the day, we all deserve love and a chance to be phenomenal. God loves you, Stephanie loves you, and you need to love yourself!

ABOUT THE AUTHOR

Stephanie Sterling was born to become a successful entrepreneur. Her passion for others shines in every aspect of her life. Growing up in Greenville, South Carolina, Stephanie developed a deep love for people that translates into a protective instinct to help others on all levels. Whether she is giving advice, being a listening ear, volunteering her time to her community, or just being there for her loved ones as well as strangers she come across who needs her help and support. Driven and ambitious is something she has always been since her childhood years. Always excelling in school by making good grades, she excelled on all levels in school with little assistance. She has always been naturally gifted to be self-motivated. Stephanie strived to have the grades it would take to obtain a top-level college education, and her decision to major in business was part of her master plan to own multiple businesses. She graduated from the University of South Carolina Upstate with a BA in Business Administration and Management.

Currently Stephanie is the founder of KidzFusion, a mobile kid's fitness program designed especially for Upstate children to help them overcome obesity and other weight-related issues. Her goal is to combat childhood obesity so that in turn, it will defeat adult obesity. The plan and vision are to start locally with those she can immediately help, and eventually scale her initiatives to a much larger National level; changing the lives of children one family at a time. She volunteers her time in the community by working with nonprofit organizations such as Our Hidden Treasures Inc and other local causes.

Being a fitness instructor for kids was just the beginning. As she continues to build her legacy, being an author will open other doors for her to continue to help others not only on a National level but an International level as well. Her book, Fatherless Success, will allow her to help others who suffered from similar hardships of life due to the lack of a parent, whether a father or mother, being absent growing up. Now her story can help her empower others; and continue to be a mentor to not only children, but adults as well. Stephanie looks forward to being your support system and showing you that you are not alone in your process of healing and overcoming adversity in life.

Resources and more can be found at

www.theauthenticstephaniesterling.com

You can follow me on Facebook and Instagram

@theauthenticstephaniesterling

THE AUTHENTIC
Stephanie Sterling

Made in the USA
Middletown, DE
12 February 2023

23948788R00035